Amidst A Breakdown

Amidst A Breakdown

Aiyana DeNoyelles

Abditory PRESS

Amidst A Breakdown by Aiyana DeNoyelles.
Abditory Press 2024

ISBN: 979-8-9908256-0-4 (Paperback)
ISBN: 979-8-9908256-1-1 (eBook)

First edition: September 2024

To those who have journeyed through darkness
and whose scars are entangled
within the fibers of their very being

Table of Contents

READER NOTE

This collection of poetry aims to express often unspoken struggles of borderline personality disorder—the internal war that rages on. While BPD is a highly stigmatized disorder, those who are fighting it are not as harmful as some may portray us to be. We often are enduring an unseen, agonizing battle within ourselves. Typically, fearing the traits we are accused of. Often we try hard not to let the harsh words be true.

More times than not, it is the quick shift of emotional extremes that cause us to say or do things that appear misleading. Not because it is a lie, but because it is a true reflection of our thoughts and feelings as they arise. Please understand that we can be some of the most loving and compassionate people you will ever meet.

I wrote these poems in the darkest of times to express my own wildly complex experiences. I hope through these works people can find a better understanding to what is not readily apparent.

It is important to note that these pieces exhibit my experiences. We are all different in the ways we think and feel. While often we share similar thoughts and traumas, not everyone acts and reacts in the same ways.

I hope you enjoy these words I've written from the heart. If you relate to some of these works, just know that you are not alone.

All the best,

Content Warning: self-harm, suicidal ideation, abuse, grieving/death.

Gamboge

Dear Old Friend

The fox visits twice a day, once in the morning and
once more to make sure I'm okay.
Tears fall as I think of what may have been,
the fox lets me know that wishing is not a sin.

I love my home, my family, my place.
I love the things that fill my life day after day.
But what I miss I'll never know.
I long for knowledge of life unlived.
I plead with my dreams to show me what could have been.

The fox sits at my window, its eyes lock with mine.
Watch as time divides.
Life reflected, split to pieces
each choice, turn, and every possibility between.
The creature brings me memories, ones I would have lived if only.

The past haunts at night, I wake to rapid beating beneath my seams.
I reach to write,

Dear old friend...
However, I was never important enough to be remembered.

Aiyana DeNoyelles

TALENTLESS

The talent I possess comes as a soft gust of wind, not a blast
Those gifted with abilities strong as pounding rain impress

Thoughts of fame and fortune consumed who I used to be
Now I do not seek to master anything
To just be and experience is enough to please

The pitter-patter of soft rain drops
feels much more satisfactory
Cheering on the powerful winds
leave behind any jealousy

Grand stage lights will never blind my eyes
Acceptance of this will one day put to ease the
young child stomping in puddles
urging that I still try and succeed

Turn Back Time

Bring me to a time untold

Lay me down in bed, I might unfold
Hold me close by your side
Bring me on a day long car ride
Trace my face to help me sleep
Tell me stories I will always keep
Feed me love and words unknown

I need to remember the times untold

Aiyana DeNoyelles

We Dreamers

Most of us dreamers
had to rush from reality
Find somewhere safe outside of the confines
that threatened our existence.

This new home we found filled of fluffy clouds and
mythical legends held us tight
Guarded our hearts.

When our dreams were threatened,
to be stripped away
the sky began to fall
The new realm we crafted starts to crumble
And tears flood the kingdoms.

Us dreamers needed to
imagine a world where we could be everything we
were told and shown would be impossible to achieve.

The real world tries hard to take away our safety
But we have only survived so far
because our ability to create worlds
unlike any we will ever touch with bare feet.

Stories

I have put in place

within a hollow space

transformed before prying eyes

a conscious knowledge

Only if you desire

Peek inside

Take your time

oh, the things

you're bound to find

if you dare

read the stories

that flow there

Aiyana DeNoyelles

ALONE

There are people around
but that does not relieve our lonesome
Though side by side,
You're still alone, walking in a line of your own
Stuck in skin
trapped inside a skeleton
unable to escape
Wishing to release what is held in at bay

Only peace comes with sleep
It lulls the mind

Stolen Childhood

My body may age
And my soul may hold experience from hundreds of years
However, the persona I play
Has never aged past a specific day

Stuck in time

Frozen by the cruel icy hands of traumata,
A child who once grew too old too fast
Is now back with years lost, unable to get them back
Forced to play adult once again only to find
It's much harder the second time around
When you are finally allowed the comfort of being a kid

Aiyana DeNoyelles

Happiness

It comes as a euphoric lie

Feeling unstoppable and too high

Unable to ever die

Like a child on the playground

jumping from a swing for the first time

A feeling of bunnies nestled in your chest

Though it can also feel like a mess

Because it is a nasty lie

The happiness is not organic

You get an ounce, then chase

the rush for the rest of your life

Lie To Me

Play dumb, they say.
Don't let it take hold.
But why—why must I dwindle myself down
to something small to appease another?
I am who I am. There is no changing that fact.

If someone can not handle being who they are
and reduces interactions with false narratives,
then they are not worthy
to walk alongside me on this journey.

Aiyana DeNoyelles

Life is a merry-go-round

        A carousel of chaos

These circles we go in never stops

        Being whirled around distorts perception

Are these things in my head real

        Or fabricated illusions

When your foot leaves the platform

        How long until clarity sets in

Is it crazy to believe sanity can be achieved

Stories crafted with the utmost cleverness
An imagination fueled by anxious wonders
Once used to take me away, escape
Turned dark, vividly playing out horrible fates
An intrusion I can't escape
scenes of horrors I'd never wish
to see the light of day
Death and terror seep in
turning the once beautiful place
into dull and dreadful daydreams
a true hellscape

Aiyana DeNoyelles

Overthinking

The human brain is exhausting

It makes you want, think, and feel

Yet, I desire nothing at all.

I don't understand the tangled mess

Left confused

I can't stand that I am so bothered by things less serious

than feelings lead to believe

Trapped in a false reality conjured on my own

Spinning tales that should be left alone

Just to pick fights solely over suspicion

Is it a need to feel something a little more?

Is that why I splash paint across an already colorful wall?

When nothing is felt, numbness turns to pain—

everything hurts the same

Tears trapped inside, I wish they would fall

Sometimes the feeling of being alive

is enough to invoke dried up eyes

It drives me and everyone around mad

It took so long to understand that I share my insanity

Am I just your escape from normalcy?

I feel so much agony over things that shouldn't affect me

A shell of a person, causing havoc due to reckoning

Cerulean

Sadness

My heart taken into the palm of a hand
clutched and crushed swiftly to dust
Bones and flesh bruised to the touch
The feeling of an indescribable weight
anchoring me down
Like a flood has come and water has rushed
straight to my lungs
Sadness may feel blue to you, but to me,
it is a dark salty sea of never ending waves
making it impossible to breathe

Aiyana DeNoyelles

Puppet

To know who I am now
you must know who I was
While the past is long gone,
it lingers with every move I make

To know someone in full
you must learn all their parts
What makes them tick
comes from what once was

The years prior haunt us all
in the shadows lurking
never to allow comfort

The ghosts are puppeteering

Is This Meant To Be Fun

People never stay

I don't want to feel this ache

I wish to escape this awful place and

Let the memory of me dissipate

Sometimes I feel insane

Like it's all for nothing

A sick, twisted game

Eventually I will meet my fate

I'm fine, it's okay

I just feel a little cumbersome today

Don't miss me when I'm gone

I wasn't having any fun

There is no purpose if it must end

Do you suffer this way or am I truly unraveling?

Forgive me, but I don't want to

make it any further than this

Aiyana DeNoyelles

Amidst a Breakdown

Treasured Time

Understanding thoughts
as they play through TIME
memories unwind differently.

How I remember is not how you do,
events that occurred are obscured
some blend into others
distorting reality.

Trust you?
When I cannot trust myself...

Remnants fade
of TREASURED days.

Aiyana DeNoyelles

We laugh and joke
In the name of our hurt
The friends that dump all the
Painful experiences on the table
And poke at the details
Pushing them into little piles
To find a laugh
It's not that pain is humorous
But if it weren't funny
Then it'd be sad
Unbearable to defeat

PROTECTOR

I am my mother's protector
Though she does not know
Despite my attempt to rid her life of evil
She can't see what I do

I, my mother's protector
Love her so
Still, the nights I laid awake in puddles of tears for days
Wondering if she'd been taken away
She will never understand

I, my mother's protector
Feel hate to my core
For someone I have always adored

I, my mother's protector
Cannot hug, kiss, or utter three words
Because denial takes away the years
I lied awake in unbearable pain,
Wishing she were home or would answer the phone

Aiyana DeNoyelles

So when the fists hit
When the dishes broke
When walls cracked and hate ensued,
I would be there

To scream and kick and punch
The ones who caused harm
Still, despite my efforts, I protect under a clock
That grants invisibility
It is why she will never know

But I, my mother's protector, do not care
I will slay any beast that comes her way
Even though she may not
Know or care

To Fly Or Fall

I dream of falling from a high place
How fun it would be to fly
Climb to the top of the tallest mountain
and take a leap, soar through clouds

I've always been jealous of birds
Their freedom is profound
Hikes end in thoughts of falling
Purposefully, even though
I'd be too scared to try

Aiyana DeNoyelles

Once You've Given Trust Betrayal Will Break You

Don't trust, not a soul

All the times I've willingly put myself in danger

just to evade the numbness

I'd rather feel too immensely than not a thing

All the cars I've gotten into

Every person I've let in my mine

The strange houses I've walked through

The secret rendezvous

It sounded like fun, and it was

But it all started too young

I learned by age twelve

That I was safer in the danger of my own choosing

Because it was never as threatening

No stranger has hurt me, at least not in ways by those

I trusted with full certainty

A Piece Of Each

I am a collection of all those who came and went

Like Frankenstein's Monster of personalities

Stitched together are the interests of others

molded and crafted

A piece of everyone I've admired

created who I am

So much so that I feel I do not even

know who I am

Everything I like and dislike

stems from someone else

A concoction of those who came and went

All the things thought to make me who I am

were borrowed from those

who pulse in and out of my life

EXPECTING THE WORST EVEN WHEN THINGS ARE GOOD

I know we don't think the same
I can't seem to understand how–
how your mind doesn't twist and turn
Get caught in potholes along the way
and lead you to the conclusions I've come to
I don't understand how you can't see the lights
that blind up ahead on the road
but you don't
Maybe that's why the deer got hit
by you instead of me

I dug for days, months,

Shoveled out the dry soil

Ridding the garden of decaying roots

And you came along

Replaced the ditch with fresh dirt

Although you dumped all your love

into my self made grave

The flowers never grew

Instead of nurturing the soil

You left the garden to rot once again

Forgot I had been digging

For what felt like a lifetime,

All that work

Undone

You trapped me in the garden bed

But no one determines another's fate

I claw to the top

Emerging with vengeance

To live another day

Or dig another hole without

Your false hope

Aiyana DeNoyelles

When Love Dies

What is love to be called when it fades away?
Does it drift from your heart and linger in empty space?
Love dies and causes breaking inside.

Does it hurt worse when it is torn from the internal?
I feel the cracks in my heart. Why must it break?

What is it called when your heart turns cold?
No words to help fathom,
almost like you're lost in the snow
one day numb to the ache of hypothermic heartbreak.

What does love become after it dies?
Adrift into a void or on a search for another to bury inside.
How do you describe the destruction when light leaves your eyes
and your heart loses the meaning to life?

Can you continue to thrive
when love dies, after we survive ?

Should we hold tight to the pain in hopes brighter days
may emerge from dismay?

Belong

rose, thorn

sun, warmth

sky, stars

pond, frog

plant, soil

heart, yours

All the things that do belong

home, happy

bed, safe

blanket, cozy

tea, honey

All the things that do belong

Thorns hurt, but roses are lovely. The sky shines with stars light.

The sun beams warmth upon bare skin.

Frogs hop around ponds croaking till dawn.

Plants sprout from beneath the soil.

Home is a feeling when something familiar is close.

And all these words are meaningless apart,

but together they belong. Much like my heart when you are gone.

Aiyana DeNoyelles

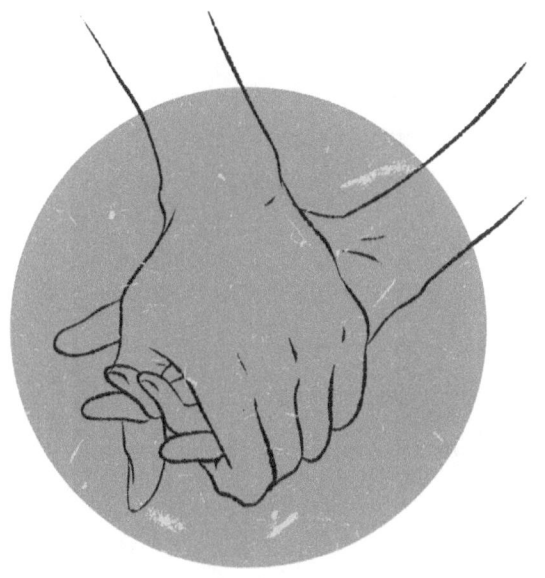

Amidst a Breakdown

The way love is described
in books, movies, by those who
have been together all their lives
invokes fear that I'll never feel it
The love I've known was never real
Lust and love blur together
unable to tell them apart
It begins with lust, turns to obsession
And just when I think I've found love
the intense feelings flee
And I'm unable to determine if what took over
my every thought resided outside reality
Or if love is truly a calm that isn't
as magnificent as we've been led to believe

Aiyana DeNoyelles

Foolish Engagement

one night, one time
countless looks
a facade, so sublime
stolen bond
not a bind
wavering, conned
enraptured by
manipulative lines
an eccentric lifeline

a jumbled mess
  how tragic to leave
    someone you wanted
      in such distress

When Our Strings Tangle

In the bar you couldn't peel your eyes from mine
I moved your way and brushed right by
Bought you a drink because I knew
you would show up by my side

A tall, muscular, jock type
I'm not too fond of men with brown eyes
but I could've lost my mind looking into yours
I wanted so desperately for you to love me
even though I met you that night

Your string knotted with mine
You bare your soul to me
in return, I let you get close

I drove you home and
we got married in the living room
Your roommates loved me
even though I wasn't your type
and you certainly were not mine

You confessed so much and in return
I showed you my softest side the
one I hide from most others

Aiyana DeNoyelles

Then the next day we planned a real date
I thought just maybe you might
have been my soulmate
but you faded away

I still see you every time I go to
that place our strings tangled
like fate and destiny working together

I thought maybe our strings were
one and the same

You smile my way
knowing you abandoned our great love story
Maybe that is why the glances
began to dissipate
our eyes don't make contact anymore

And I am left to wonder
why you went through all the trouble

In this dream, you were everything to me.

A shred of something I never knew was possible to receive.

For that, I should be grateful and caring.

Instead, I became all the things I've always despised.

You deserve more than I could ever be.

My Favorite

All the power you hold
you don't even realize the control
Whatever you want I'll do
for only you
You're dangerous to be around
I can't stay away, I need to hear
your voice, see your face
You predict my moods
Control every hope and dream
I've had many favorite people
But slowly they become insufferable
Once gone, I miss them for years
maybe forever, but pieces of me hate
each and every one so much
for taking advantage of the hold they had

TRUST SO FRAGILE

Think of the possibilities...
a life that could blossom between you and I,
the beautiful, endless world that we could share.
Secrets I could finally release from the dark depths they hide away in
to be placed in your heart, knowing you would keep safe
all my dearest and darkest thoughts.

Safe from my own dysfunctional mind,
but if I spoke those words, I long to set free
Would you still want me?

Are you even mine?

Could I trust you with the most fragile bits of my tattered soul?
Would knowledge lead to destruction?
If I told you I never desired for anything more,
would you make space in your heart for the love that I could pour?
Would it come flowing back,
or would you seal it away—stolen selfishly,
never to be reciprocated?

Aiyana DeNoyelles

Captive Fervor

Your eyes sear mine

as I search for a way to

cascade the words encapsulated

where river turns to waterfall

Yet none become vocal

A dam stands in the way

So much to express and reveal

Unable to let the water flow naturally

A trickle if lucky

All these intense emotions

cause rapids to form

yet I never know if I have ever truly felt love

A Childish Game

Meaningless mumbles with no fruition flood closed ears

Caused by twisting thoughts and conflicting emotions

they leave my mouth, float around, and disappear

You stare at me as if you need to hear my words

as if you cannot see the hurt displayed on my face

How am I to find direction when you wont

release your true thoughts instead of hate

Maybe the evil venom you spew is the truth

And I am nothing to you

then why don't you leave

Is it because you know the control you have over me?

Aiyana DeNoyelles

Split To Easily

Screaming and fights

Night after night

"I hate you"

"You are nothing to me"

But when you turn to leave

Something inside cracks

I fall involuntarily and beg on my knees

The tears flood

"I love you"

"You can't leave"

"I need you"

"Don't you love me?"

I thought being at war meant we

were in love, but

after all we've been through

you seem so unfazed

If Only I Could Promise Forever

You whisper forever gently in my ear
"I love you, forever"

How could anyone envision such a task
To stay by the side of insanity
To endure the torture that comes from
Knowing someone so haunted

Forever never meant what I believed it to be
Forever is not a long time
But something fleeting
Which only lasts on the condition that I appear stable

But when you say forever,
I feel you mean it, though I cannot be sure
I have felt that way too often before
Time will tell, but it's time I do not wish to endure
Once again waiting for someone to love
Not just me, but the devil that I can be

Aiyana DeNoyelles

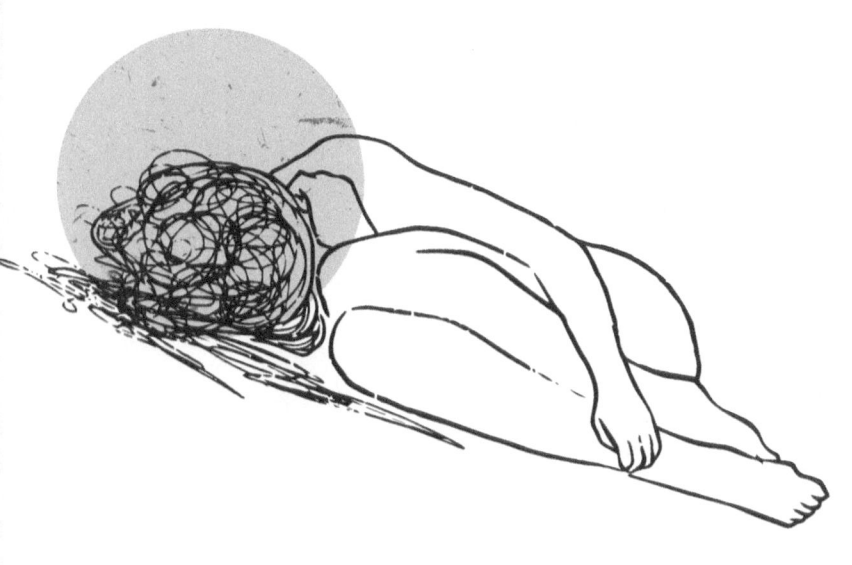

I'll Leave First

Your passion unravels before my eyes

Slowly, over time, like the thread on my favorite sweater

worn one too many times

Your passion felt fiery, unlike any I'd ever experienced

Maybe that is what made me want to love you

But the flames have died down

I thought you'd love me forever

Scorching the earth with every touch

I think it's time for me to go

Before your heart becomes fully undone

and you realize I'm not the one

But I can't

If you say it first, then I can hate

But I must be the one to seal our fate

I crave the love I've missed my whole life

If you don't want to be bonded for all eternity

I will take my leave, just not without a fight

Not because I want to, but because

I cannot leave without disaster raging around me

I have ended beautiful things to see if I could feel

I've stayed through horrid storms because I felt too much

There is no way of knowing what was real

I travel on with the knowledge of

my own self crafted downfall

I Don't Wish You Well

I haven't been able to listen to
my favorite band for years now
You've ruined that for me
and it's fine
I don't need to hear those songs
That once brought joy, then suffering
I don't care for the flashbacks the music brings
I just hope every time you hear that riff
you lay awake at night
reliving everything you ever did
And find yourself unable to shut your eyes
Consumed by guilt and self hatred

Aiyana DeNoyelles

A hand that doesn't quite fit in another as it used to

A heart which no longer skips a beat

A mind that has grown too big for its home

Like a puzzle piece left out in the humidity

Warped by weather

The evolution of things incomplete

Crimson

Rage

fury seethes inside

it is always there

tiny bubbles of anger waiting to pop

like little landmines ready to explode from

the smallest of things in a moment's notice

My body engulfed by flames of internal ache

Every organ, every bone set ablaze

Emotional pain has never come without physical strain

My body breaks, though not visibly

Both feel one and the same

Aiyana DeNoyelles

I find myself in questionable positions
Around disreputable people
Infatuated with less than moral beings
Humans that take and drain
every last drop of affection I saved

I've learned why–
Why I can never stay still
Why I love those who don't feel
Why I do things so spontaneously
It's simple, really

I am chasing home
But the home I make haste to
was something most would run from
And the next time I'll be home is when I'm in hell
But if I find it before my time
It won't take long to get there

The cloud of sadness evolves to
an eruption of anger
I cause mayhem
you yell, threaten
display contempt

All for being the person
you sculpted me to be

This fusion of natural disaster
Didn't manifest out of nowhere

Aiyana DeNoyelles

ENERGY SPENT

Can you trust the monsters inside your head
I know I can't
If I did, I'd be dead

Cage them up in chains with locks
they taunt you to let them out
using all your life to hold them at bay
slowly rotting inside to out
in an attempt to make it through more days

Comfort From Chaos

The fighting begins, I'm not involved
just outside looking in
I freeze
not due to fear
But I'm basking in the past coming back
Loud screams and sporadic pounces
Knuckles to drywall
It calms me to a panic
Flinging objects into skulls
Morbid as is
I watch and reminisce
When my heart is in my throat,
and I am frozen
all of my homes play through
my mind like a finger is
stuck on the button that rewinds
As someone tugs and says "Come on, let's go"
I'm confused as to why
The argument will stop, and the party will revive
But I sense their fear
and I remember my sister clutching my side
or holding on to my grandma tight
I recall that I am not normal and this is not right

Aiyana DeNoyelles

They Were Meant To Help Not Make It Worse

Flashing lights ingrained in my mind

Blue and red

Doors kicked in one too many times

Handcuffs and static

Rushing outside

Suits and paperwork

Speaking words, but they think I lie

Alone in a room

At home, at school

Ambushed

By strange people who want me to

Confess something untrue

I scream in frustration

I'm scared they will make me

Leave without you

Their faces linger to this day

They never take the bad people away

But continue to invade

Causing more harm

Without any shame

I'm Sorry Even If I Don't Say It

My bones ache at the thought of apologizing
Even as I shudder at pain I've inflicted
each word, lead on my tongue.

Maybe I cannot say I'm sorry
Because no one ever showed me how
it should be done.

Stitches won't hold my wounds shut and
your heart screams for help
to close the ones I've caused
And despite that
I can't let the words escape my mouth.

Aiyana DeNoyelles

Longing To Be A Priority

Left waiting so many times
out in the cold my fingers turned numb
How often must I be pushed aside
by too many people, I've finally lost count
Your lack of care hits harder than an icy ball of snow
My essence withers away like slush melting in the rain
I can barely sense myself drift away
I pull at my hair
Bang my head into walls
Punch my thigh so many times
the skin has turned raw
And yet, I still try
as seconds drift by I've lost all sense
as to why I spent so long attempting
to be of significance in your life

The things I have done just for fun
aren't typically what you'd think of
Harmful acts in the name of excitement

These things I do are cloaked by intrigue
Wrap a cord around my neck just to know
how long it takes before I cannot breathe
Bleed for the sake of knowing
how long the stream may run
Confess my love to anyone
even those I only met once
to learn how easy it is to discard lust

The purpose is not to live with anguish for
sometimes it mends the numb
But more often than not,
it just sounded like fun

Aiyana DeNoyelles

Don't Forgive Never Forget

Forgiving is no easy feat
I think I have, but then
the anger seeps back in
like boiled water in my veins

Long after harm had been done
I convince myself that I forgave
In order for peace
you're told to forget

Forgetting is even more complex
Pain lingers as if still fresh
How can I forgive and forget
when what happened to me
has turned my heart cold

You Conjured This Villain

Remember how you locked me away
hidden in your tower, never to be seen
It wasn't like a princess story

Remember how you made your family suffer
for trying to set me free
Kept me dull with poison apples
so the dragon could feed

My mom came to get me
but yours wouldn't let her
Luxuries exchanged for compliance
don't you remember

Remember when you shattered my phone
And that time you pushed me into the road
Even with an audience the cruelty pursued
You didn't care who saw or knew

Still I believed you would one day
care about me and we would continue happily

Aiyana DeNoyelles

I escaped, of course, a few times that is
Climbed down the tower confused and bruised
With help from knights in shining armor
but none were chivalrous, just taking me away
for their own gain

No better than you

Who once slit their flesh open in front of me
forced to watch you bleed
just so I wouldn't leave, it wasn't my fault
Still you blamed me
There's much more that happened
but some secrets aren't meant to be freed

I always wanted to be a fairytale princess
I just wish I knew the horrid truths
the tales hid between the text

I was already defeated and weak
but you caused me to turn villainous

I'm not the princess of this story, I am the evil queen

CRAZY AS THEY MADE ME

You called me crazy and for that
I tore your heart out
Showed you the true meaning
You crushed me like a dried leaf
fallen from a dehydrated tree
And for that, I picked up the remainder
of your bones to build my throne
A vulture that feeds off
those who caused me to become
crazy like they called me

Aiyana DeNoyelles

Me Against Myself

Myself and I are not one in the same

It may not seem possible

but we share this space

I have a friend in here with me

no, an enemy

Often cramped and confined

we fight

I scream just in hopes to survive

But there is a mellow hiss

of my own voice

I try to convince myself

to play dangerous, unruly games

but I fight back and maim

Constant war unfolds inside my brain

My Mind Hates Us Both

I am a victim of my mind,
and you are too.
We are both held prisoner
by the demon that takes hold.
It can waltz right through the palisade.

I am a victim of my mind, you are too,
Both constrained by the same entity,
elusive to the venom seeped and stained,
Yet, no escape.

The evil tells a tale that I will never prevail,
The evil that continuously paints you
to appear as my enemy.

Sometimes it all feels very true,
although, I know you are not
as malicious as I seem to believe.
You're kind and loving to other people,
just not to the demon

that is me...

Aiyana DeNoyelles

Amidst a Breakdown

The Beast

There is something within

It lurks through darkness

Awaiting mortal sins

Terror feeds the belly

Fueling its existence

Ungodly yet all powerful

Walls built topple

Fear allows it to break through

Protect is all it knows how to do

conquer is its only goal

Destroy

Anything that hinders its host's control

Created in chaos

Birthed in tumult

Molded by upheaval

The beast breathes, sleeping

The beast waits peacefully

within

me

Aiyana DeNoyelles

It Is Of My Own Doing

I've come to find comfort in the pain
I don't think anything can ever heal the parts of my heart
that were etched away with a rusty blade

When all is calm, I am driven to insanity
Peeking around corners and waiting for the next tragedy

Once mayhem finally arrives,
A sense of sanity sets in

Though the actions of others are not mine
I can't help but wonder
Is it I who brings about the strain

A seeker of wild disarray
Forged by hellish flames,
The deranged don't find me

I call them to come and play

Viridian

I'd Kill The Reaper If I could

Death and I are not friends
intertwined once again
for some reason unknown
it seems he will never let me go
I'd vanquish him, but he never gets that close
Defeat death and live happily

Death and I are not alike
He takes and takes sacred life
Death and I have never seen eye to eye
He lingers near by hoping to
pluck someone else from my life
and break me for another time

Death and I will meet again
another encounter I could do without
I'd kill him if I could but
death is inevitable
something I have animosity toward

Aiyana DeNoyelles

Endings

To describe the feeling of saying goodbye
Is an impossible task
There is a unique sting
Almost like being stung by a bee
When a special thing comes to an end

The last episode
The end of a song
A friends departure
Fading love
Moving out

It is a specific cruelness
Which illicit hurt
Like the sting of a bee
It can't be describe simply

SOMETIMES DENIAL IS SURVIVAL

I miss you everyday
Sometimes I pretend you exist far away
Font and center for others
You're all I think about most days

I miss you more as time goes by
When the tears come flooding,
I'm never prepared

I see your face when I lay to sleep at night
Sometimes I pretend you're still here
Just to keep the sorrow from invading

Aiyana DeNoyelles

I Couldn't Forget Even If I Wanted To

The wind reminds me of a friend, it reminds me of her smile
As the breeze brushes past my face, I'm filled with
melancholic reminiscences

As she left, sun turned to shade
Nature fell to its knees
Providing a trigger for memories
The wind reminds me of that day
Leaves swirl, conjuring thoughts which once were lost
A friend who will never fade

She will never truly go away
In my heart forever, she'll stay

The wind reminds me of distant days
it reminds me of her wild ways
The wind rushes past me and the chill fades
I am embraced by warmth of better days

my

heart

crumbles

knowing I will never see you again

brings in a sadness like no other

unsure how to go on

I wish for the end

Aiyana DeNoyelles

Isn't It Quite Cruel

Only a world so cruel as this
takes lives so young
ones beautiful, ready to bloom.
A God that can claim what is his
too early, before being appreciated.

Too soon, unable to expand,
no time to plant seeds
along the paths they've woven.
To die before a chance to
learn beyond what is known.
Why have a life
if the end always looms

GRIEVING

Tortured by death
Enveloped by pain
The feeling fades
but you are never quite the same

Tormented every waking day
Try hard not to let the
memories go as they slowly fade

Grief bubbles over
once again, a feeling takes over
more than frustration
filled with love and hate

how could you leave so soon,
there was so much left for us to do

Aiyana DeNoyelles

MORBID BEAUTY

A drop, so deep, salty scent in the wind
Tantalizing waves tumble and crash, rapid.
A path I fear laid out before my eyes—
The ground beneath me shakes,
legs give in and quake.
      Surrender
Blue, gray, and white splash up the side
What a beautiful view to submit to.
Violent waves rush over your grave.
Thoughts of us tangle
Cold rocks lay beneath
Who am I if you're not here?
I wish I didn't have to
but nothing makes sense alone at the shore
Could it be that cruel... departing, disappearing
just to stay close to you
Drift away with one last breath before
it leaves my chest, eyes closed
I move to take the leap
but the waves don't accept my plea
It's not my time
Stay close, I won't be late.

Afterlife

I have to believe in something great, beyond time and space
Without that, you are gone for good
never to be within my presence, to be graced with your essence,
and I would have no faith.

I have to believe I will see them all again
one day in another life, in the beyond,
not another face, though I hope to recognize your soul

I have to believe I will remember our time after I am dead and gone
I want to know I am back with you when the light fades
Don't forget us while you're in a better place

Surrounded by love

My heart does not mend together

I'll need glue maybe thread

My grandma is immortal

It has to be true

No one has ever brought comfort

To my heart more than her

She was always there

The only one who never left

The one who would face anything

Just to protect us

I fear the day she does go

It will be the thing

I don't ever recover from

This I know

Aiyana DeNoyelles

Memory is weird

I can't remember a damn thing

And somehow I remember all to much

Most of which I would give anything

To forget in an instant

Aiyana DeNoyelles

Haunting The Haunted

i used to blame myself—maybe i still do
everything bad being my fault, that's nothing new
newly fifteen, he was twenty-two
our crowds easily mixed and mingled
but that's no good excuse

blinded by feelings of being hated
i ignored the odious truth that loomed
i wasn't stupid—or maybe so

flashbacks of our adventures,
late night drives, bonfires, hikes
it all seemed so grand back then
and then he went and died
i used to imagine his ghost lingering nearby
i still sit at his grave
but these days that might be out of hate
despite it all, i miss him every day
because i never got the chance to explain
how much i'm filled with hate

it seems he does still haunt me
just not in the way he used to

I'm Still Your Friend

I've come to know so many people along the way
Some shared bonds so strong

Support and show love to the people
I've collected through the years
But they never seem to do the same

I always seem to be pushed aside,
easily forgotten, and often overlooked

My accomplishments don't shine a bright enough light
Yet I continue to love those same people

Curious as to why they mean so much to me
when I am nothing but a ghost haunting from behind the scenes

Aiyana DeNoyelles

Hurt and fear erupt

Spews volcanic ash

Judgment obscured

In the smog

The truth is obvious

But I can't let it be

Fight to rationalize

Though logic always flees

Someone new has crafted the

Volcano inside

They take up pieces of your life

Gaps I once filled

But now my spots are shared

And soon they will force me away

I beg you not to leave

Don't worry you repeat

CALL IT HOME

Some people have childhood rooms
they get to go back to as they age
They wander a house they've known for decades
and as time goes by, the memories stay ingrained
As they walk the staircase and through hallways
just as they did as kids

I will never know such a beautiful experience

From house to house, none became home
Some demolished, some converted
And when I pass by once in a while
I remember the times contained in those walls
most tragic, but some pleasant

A home is not a painted box, yet I will never
have one to wander and reminisce
Something so many take for granted

Aiyana DeNoyelles

Obsidian

Woken Up

Consciousness granted years ago

Placed in a body at twelve years old

finally woken

gifted with lucidity

Feels more like a curse

To be outside watching who you are said to be, trail along

Then one day given control

of a human body

Forced to live within an already defeated soul

An ache to drop the reins takes hold

Wasted Time

I could waste my time wondering
Thoughts overpowered by all the whys,
but I've come not to mind.
I've known more fathers than most.
Each leaving me with at least one cherished memory.

I could waste my time wondering
where the good memories with you have gone,
but there were none to have forgotten in the first place
Even themes filled with fun—splattered red with pain

I could waste my time wondering why.
I didn't ask to know you. It's what you wanted,
then you let your family distort me.
Allowed them to infect until
you painted me pitch black, lost to darkness.
But I was a child—
Crafted to be horrid and hopeless.
The fact is you, an adult
could not bear to hear the truth from the child
you chose then deemed wasn't worthy of you.

Peace and happiness, something I cannot wish.

Delusions Of The Righteous

I remember the twinge of fingers around my throat
How it stayed sore
like phantom hands
loitering in my space
How they said I'd end up like my mother
as if that were a horrible fate
And how they went to church the Sunday after
Gloating is their favorite game

A Christian
No... a wolf in sheep's clothing
Hiding behind religion to pretend they're good
But I know the sins that stain pristine fingertips
And I know their God would be disappointed
So I pray they are never forgiven

Out of all the ones who stole a shred of my soul
This one hurt the most

Aiyana DeNoyelles

"Take this pill, you'll feel better," she said

By 9:00 am I was off venturing through wonderland

By 11:00 am I thought I might be dead

Almost overdosed, I learned some time ago

The contents of my stomach came up

all over a history test, the whole class got a pass

Funny how the teacher told me to find a change of clothes

How could they not know? It was obvious

I called my mother crying, she made me feel better

She wanted to pick me up from school, but I wouldn't let her

The dragon was mad, "How dare you get high without me"

I cried into his shoulder,

"I thought it was Tylenol, that's what she told me."

By 3:00 pm I called my mom again, "I still feel weird," I said

She told me what she suspected I took

I couldn't believe my friend would drug me

She did it a lot actually, others would do the same

I learned how someone else's life was just a game

A heart black impure
Depleted to desolate dust
Once worthy of love

Aiyana DeNoyelles

I once believed I deserved it

That you were karma on a mission

our

hate

brewed

from

desire

you

did

this

to us

Riddled our fake love with detest

Your name now tastes of blood on my breath

A Heart Cursed

A storm brews deep within.

The embodiment of peace that once swirled

around like eddies dwindles leaving a void darker than an abyss.

She, who was once filled with love and light,

had the daisies ripped from her heart,

only to be replaced by thorn plagued vines.

A heart that once poured tons of pure tenderness

now oozes buckets of detest.

Struck down one too many times.

Her eyes turn dull, no passion to be found,

Her tongue sharpened to spew only the cruelest of sounds.

No one will step on her heart again, and if they dare do so,

the thorns encasing it will pierce skin, infecting the culprit

with the pain she endured from loving

without caution and caring all too genuine.

Aiyana DeNoyelles

I want to go home I scream
Time and time again
Even when within the four walls
I had lived the longest

I want to go home I cry
But nothing
And no one
Fills the vacancy
No matter how comfortable, safe, or familiar

There is no home for me
I've come to believe
That spot in my heart will forever
Rest hollow
I'll never know what it feels like to be at peace

A Shift In The Season

flowers bloom and then color fades

something we watch on repeat

one petal falls another flew away

the world changes to gray

a gloom, a daze

I am not okay

the false reality stripped away

a descent to devilry

starts once sanity strays

Aiyana DeNoyelles

ISOLATE

I've done it again
Cut myself off from civilization
Not left the house in months
Haven't answered any texts
Or participated in events

I was once kept away by
Dragons and selfish rescuers
But now I've become the thing
I longed to escape

I lock myself away
Unable to find the will to flee

But you can't run from yourself

Simply Suffering

Deep within the darkest walls of my mind,
I sit without a thought to consume the everlasting decay.
Trapped inside memories of days that came and went away.
The world passes by as I stay stuck inside my troublesome mind.

Time ticks on, yet I am nowhere in sight.
Hiding behind sullen eyes.
If one could crawl through the maze that is my brain
and take my place—relieve my aches.
I would wander far beyond the melancholy confinement
that holds me hostage from seeing the light.

So take my hand, guide me through, lead the way home
let me stay, rest for more than one night.
Teach me to live without the pain that I inflict.

Listen to music, how the sound invigorates lives.
Maybe one day that will include mine.

While I wither in a hollow shell filled with unnecessary agony,
inspired to come to life, but just for a moment.
Falsified hope—nothing good heads this way
I wither away hidden inside my dark, decaying mind.

Aiyana DeNoyelles

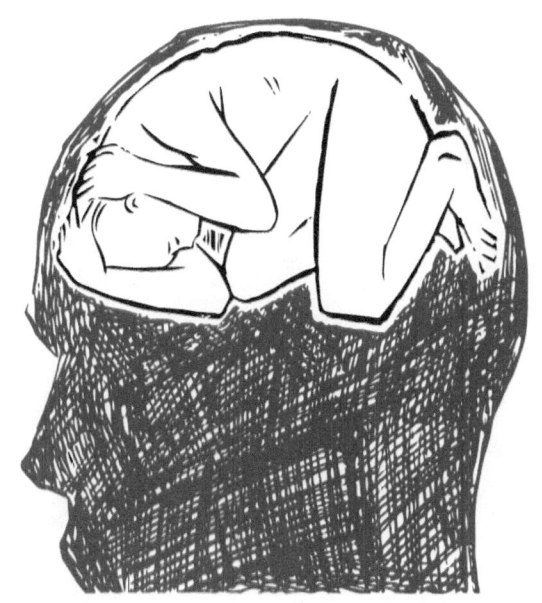

Amidst a Breakdown

Dissociate

My consciousness feels
like a baseball bat has been
swung too hard
Hard enough to shatter the fragile glass
that encased my sentience
the glass that kept my mind safe

Consciousness rolls in
being torn apart by
punctures from small shards
I've been pulled out of
the vitrine only to be smothered
by a dark, twisted reality

Aiyana DeNoyelles

Fear

Have you ever fallen asleep and fell in your dream
only to wake up to your body quake
and the bed shake beneath

Fear feels a bit like that to me
A rush of uncertainty
Constantly scanning for danger
behind a closed door or out of the corner of my eye,

Fear is anxiety mixed with paranoia and it hardly ever leaves
When I fear, I react dramatically
It feels as though you are in a dark forest,
surrounded by vicious creatures
worse than you could dream
waiting to pounce the moment you blink

Often a voice whispers, "give up"
I want to listen
To stop the torment
This endless cycle
of trying and failing

"Just give up," I murmur
But a higher power wont let me, I can't
The whispers become like nails on
a chalkboard the more they are ignored

The whisper sighs like wind
through leaves at midnight
"Why not end the suffering?"
It makes sense, too much sense
Why continue to choose this

Because I am foolish
And hope is for fools
with nothing to lose

Aiyana DeNoyelles

I am not as small as I feel or you may think

I will never stand for misery to crowd when

It hasn't been brought on by my own suffering

I take no pleasure in our quarrel

Still I revel as your crown falls

Escape

I lay at night as my mind flashes through thoughts of things
I cannot begin to fathom as fast as they arise.
The walls loom over as I shift in bed, locked,
no—trapped
inside the darkest corners of my head.
Waiting to cry, nothing comes out
I am numb to the pain that floats about the rivers of regret.
The world watches as I suffer silently in anguish,
masking my misery from prying eyes,
if only to avoid the pity and snide remarks
of those that don't know what it is like to feel so utterly alone.

I miss the days of happiness that never drifted away.
The times I could sit and lull to sweet symphonies,
my internal thoughts would play.
But now I sit with nothing but shame, wishing
for something beautiful to float my way.
decaying as smiling faces turn this way,
I can barely make it through one full day.
Just once please, I plead with myself,
"Life is misery," I whisper to a void on repeat.
As I drift away, the bane of being held captive
by my own existence is comical in a way.

Aiyana DeNoyelles

Nothing stops me from feeling so hopeless—helpless.

The pills, the doctors, the endless soothing

used to drown out the child in pain,

they do nothing to rid me of the torment.

Lingering stings created by the demons that lurk within my brain.

I try, I do, I want to live my life greatly; I swear I do.

But what will save me from myself

when all I do is revert to what I once knew.

Hate to be this way, fighting myself endlessly—

energy comes but quickly fades faster and faster every time

I do something other than let myself deteriorate.

Constant obsession over things insignificant crowd my brain,

all the factors that regularly haunt my waking hours,

aimlessly wandering through a horrific daydream,

the essence of it all is so hard to explain.

Sometimes I am perfectly sane,

others I am a rat begging to be let out of the maze.

Released from the grip of thoughts for just one moment,

so I can regain all the wonderful things brought upon

by what feels to be a long ago dream,

I may have never actually been there to witness.

Nightmares

The horrors that sneak in at night

Are not of creatures that lurk

But of the monstrous beings that walk in plain sight

There are terrors in life which some can't fathom

Despite the bubble unable to burst

Despite how much they refuse

I have lived them

The monsters may never come for you

I wish that to be true

But don't be a fool

I once believed they couldn't get me too

They exist alongside our every move

Aiyana DeNoyelles

I'm scared of so much now
can barely step outside alone
I don't understand,
I survived,
Time after time

When I'm in a panic
I remind myself I never died
I am immortal,
it's a lie, I know
but pieces of me believe it
I should've been dead many years ago

Aiyana DeNoyelles

At times I expose too much truth
too soon, too blatant
Yet not nearly enough

I'm much more comforted by lies
Concealing the facts
Spinning a story with craft
in order to contort because
If I say it enough times, I can
begin to believe I'm normal, I am fine,
not a victim too many times

Though a look inside my mind
must be honest

Everything ruined too often
by allowing the raw emotions
to push through
Nobody really wants
to hear something as
mundane as what is true
Not even me who subconsciously
knows the truth

The Girl Who Cried One Too Many Times

Each word jagged and sharp, voices CRESENDO in dissonance
A crashing clatter of screams, fill her ears as tears fall
She hides behind the dog—she holds him tight, never to let go
But HE let her dog die, and her heart cried another time

When the voices rose once again, CRESENDOING without end
No dog to hide behind, she lost her best friend
She played her music loud to drown them out
But when she heard a yelp, her throat grew tight
Her heart beat fast, CLANGING of symbols in her ears too loud
Her feet flew to the commotion

Stopped in her tracks, she lurked
Imagining morbid ways to stop the attacks

The girl cried and cried
And one day it was one too many times
For no tears would fall, her eyes were dry
To used to the world being so cruel
She bathed in jagged words, consumed by TRAGEDY
Becoming one with the darkness, trapped with no way out

Aiyana DeNoyelles

I don't know if
things are truly as
therapeutic as people say

I feel the same way
I tell them I don't think I'll ever change
Not because I don't want to
I just don't think it is a possibility

Every time I feel healed
I start to spin out again

Lavender

You don't realize addiction is afoot
It slithers up your body
Making stops along the way to the top
Wraps itself around your throat
Only do you realize when it bites
And teeth puncture the jugular

The work begins when
The venom seeps into too deep
And you finally realize
You are not okay

Aiyana DeNoyelles

Waiting For You

The wisdom you seek will only appear soon after you digest

Release all cares, brave the path you walk

It will lead you exactly to where

serenity lingers, but only when you make it through

will tranquility be waiting

A Journey To Heal

When I close my eyes and darkness takes over the light,

a little bright patch remains

giving room to escape, to chisel away

The darkness makes me weak

I long to pick at the seams—

piece by piece, the way you peel chipped paint

Life is a twisting, winding brush stroke

unsure where to go or if there will a hole in the canvas

eating away at sanity

Small bits of darkness flake away

But someone comes and fills the space back in

conflict invades the calm

Laying back in your place

a thought invades

why become better when I could simply hide forever

But the paint will chip again and one day the light will rush in

every crack lit, slowly expanding the breaking points

filling us with hope, shattering a shell once created by torment

bursting through the hard exterior, emerges

the new you,

the loved you

Aiyana DeNoyelles

She Is Part Of Me

I've tried to shut her up
But she doesn't stay quiet for long
When something goes wrong she pops back up
And taunts me with a sour song

Sometimes I wish I could flee
To not live with the person I can be
But we are one and the same
Without her there is no me

You must tend to the wilted garden
Rather than wait for the ground to freeze

Refresh

Breathe in the summer dew
Breathe out the winter chill
Breathe in the sun that shines
Let out the darkness inside

Only you can mend your mind
Breathe in the things that keep you alive
Breathe out the pain provoking cries

Inhale laughter and joy
Exhale all the lies that haunt your mind
Inhale the hope of all who survived
Exhale each and every worry, set them aside

Keep in mind you are still alive
Release everything that may have convinced you otherwise
Remind yourself of a future in which you don't want to die

Aiyana DeNoyelles

The Past

How do you let go of the past when it is all you think about

How do you forget all of the things that shaped you

How do you let go and live on

How do you stop wondering

who you would've been if none of it happened

How

      How

            How

The answer is different for everyone

I'm still searching for clues

Looking for a way to take the images of horrible things away

One day

      One day

            One day

Everything will be okay in some way

With time we will all find our ability to be free

Free

      Free

            Free

From the agony

blowing winds rush
overhead moonlight
glistening down
the forest whispers sweet songs
yet with the sharpest of tongues
"don't go in, doom awaits"
one foot after the other
closer to the unseen
closing in on the veil between
here and there
"turn back now"
but another path appears
an option you haven't thought
wander through the fog
off the dark trail
down the now one
think of all the possibilities
who knows maybe
that could be the way home

Aiyana DeNoyelles

One Day

Some stories are too complex, too harmful to tell
I am learning they are mine and I'm allowed to share
I have more tales to expel
More monsters to expose
And one day
I will
Without fear

That is part of healing
it needs to be

ACKNOWLEDGEMENTS

I want to give a huge thank you to those who contributed in traumatizing me enough to the point of writing poetry.

But seriously, I have people to thank.

Jenna, for being such a great friend to me and such a huge encouragement to continue my journey as a writer. Kaydee, for being my go to when I need logical advice—cover design, proofreading, editing, pretty much everything. But more importantly, for putting up with my nonsense for years. Terran, who was such a kind human and gave me the most amazing feedback for cover design despite having met only recently. This story wouldn't have the cover it does without them. My partner, for being supportive and helping me to continue following my dreams. The sensitivity readers, for making sure I accomplished what I set out to do with this book. A big thank you to the ARC team. Without your help, this little poetry collection would have no shot. And the street teams help, so I'm not yelling into a void, hoping someone would take interest. And most importantly, the biggest thank you of all is to my cats. They didn't actually do anything except yell at me when it was food time.

Thank you so much for reading.

If you enjoyed this collection please consider leaving a review.

Ratings and reviews are extremely helpful in many ways and much appreciated.

Aiyana DeNoyelles is an author and artist from New York. Reading has always been the perfect escape from reality, offering endless adventure. Through books, Aiyana quickly discovered that she was not alone in her experiences and hopes to share that sense of connection and solace with readers.

Aiyana is diagnosed with a few mental health disorders including borderline personality disorder. Their poems began as a way to express complicated feelings. As she learned more about herself and others with similar diagnoses, her writing became a means to articulate what many experience but have a hard time voicing.

Find more at aiyanadenoyelles.com